OXFORD FREE PUBLIC LIBRARY
339 MAIN STREET
OXFORD, MA 01540

Amazing Archaeology

Petra

by Julie Murray

Dash!
LEVELED READERS
An Imprint of Abdo Zoom • abdobooks.com

Dash!
LEVELED READERS

Level 1 – Beginning
Short and simple sentences with familiar words or patterns for children who are beginning to understand how letters and sounds go together.

Level 2 – Emerging
Longer words and sentences with more complex language patterns for readers who are practicing common words and letter sounds.

Level 3 – Transitional
More developed language and vocabulary for readers who are becoming more independent.

abdobooks.com

Published by Abdo Zoom, a division of ABDO, PO Box 398166, Minneapolis, Minnesota 55439. Copyright © 2022 by Abdo Consulting Group, Inc. International copyrights reserved in all countries. No part of this book may be reproduced in any form without written permission from the publisher. Dash!™ is a trademark and logo of Abdo Zoom.

Printed in the United States of America, North Mankato, Minnesota.
102021
012022

Photo Credits: Getty Images, iStock, Shutterstock
Production Contributors: Kenny Abdo, Jennie Forsberg, Grace Hansen, John Hansen
Design Contributors: Candice Keimig, Neil Klinepier

Library of Congress Control Number: 2021940198

Publisher's Cataloging in Publication Data

Names: Murray, Julie, author.
Title: Petra / by Julie Murray
Description: Minneapolis, Minnesota : Abdo Zoom, 2022 | Series: Amazing archaeology | Includes online resources and index.
Identifiers: ISBN 9781098226671 (lib. bdg.) | ISBN 9781644946404 (pbk.) | ISBN 9781098227517 (ebook) | ISBN 9781098227937 (Read-to-Me ebook)
Subjects: LCSH: Petra (Extinct city)--Juvenile literature. | Jordan--Antiquities--Juvenile literature. | Civilization, Ancient--Juvenile literature. | Architecture, Nabataean--Juvenile literature. | Excavations (Archaeology)--Juvenile literature. | Archaeology and history--Juvenile literature.
Classification: DDC 939.48--dc23

Table of Contents

Petra 4

History 6

Finding Petra 16

More Facts 22

Glossary 23

Index 24

Online Resources 24

Petra

Petra is an ancient city in southern Jordan. It was built more than 2,300 years ago!

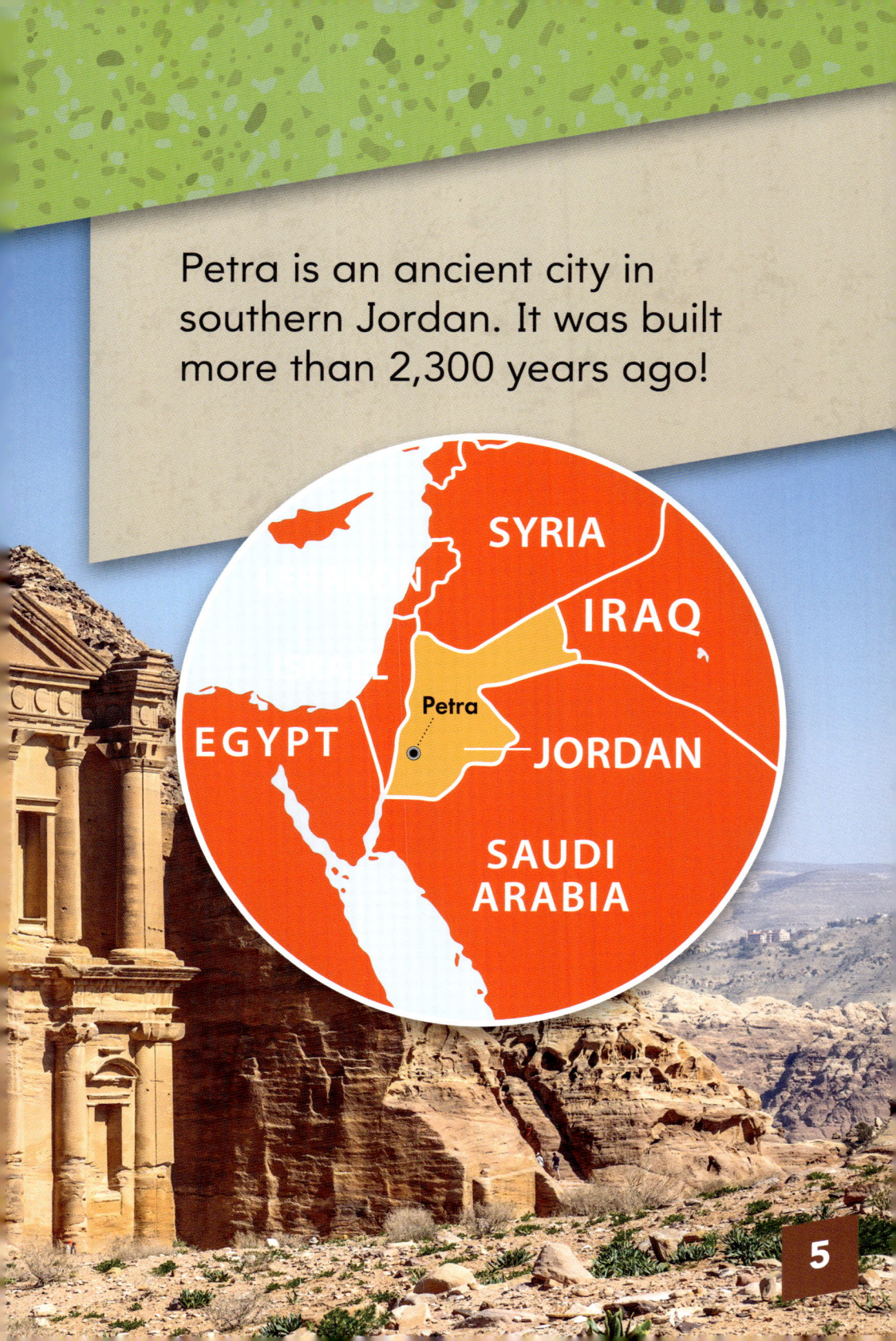

History

The Nabateans built Petra. They were wealthy desert traders and **nomads**.

Sometime before 312 BCE, they decided to settle down. The place they chose sat between the Red Sea and the Dead Sea. It was good for trade.

They carved Petra by hand into the sandstone cliffs. They covered the buildings with **stucco** and painted them bright colors.

The city had temples, theaters, and **villas**. There were also tombs and beautiful gardens.

People left Petra sometime between 300 and 400 CE. Trade routes were changing. The Nabateans moved where trade was better.

A major earthquake also struck during this time. It destroyed half of the city.

Finding Petra

The abandoned city was buried in sand over the years. On August 22, 1812, Johann Ludwig Burckhardt rediscovered Petra. He was a Swiss explorer.

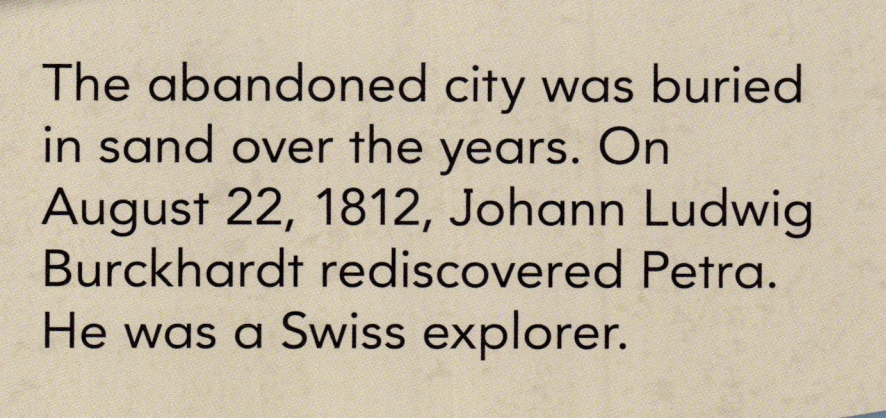

18

Archaeologists found many artifacts at the site. Statues, pottery, jewelry, and coins were just a few of the items found.

Today, people can visit the ancient city. Only about 15% of the site has been uncovered. **Archaeologists** continue to discover the wonders of Petra.

More Facts

- Petra is one of the New 7 Wonders of the World. It is also a World Heritage Site.

- Researchers believe that up to 30,000 people could have lived in Petra at one time.

- The Nabateans built an **elaborate** water collection system. It consisted of channels, canals, and dams.

Glossary

archaeologist – a scientist that digs up and then studies objects such as pottery, tools, and buildings. Archaeology is the study of past human life.

elaborate – planned or carried out with great care and attention to details.

nomad – a member of a group or tribe that has no fixed home and moves from place to place.

stucco – a durable, rough material applied while wet to exterior walls.

villa – a luxurious home.

Index

artifacts 19

buildings 12

Burckhardt, Johann Ludwig 17

Dead Sea 8

design 10

discovery 17

earthquake 15

gardens 12

Jordan 5

Nabateans 7, 8, 10, 14

Red Sea 8

rock 10

visitors 21

Online Resources

To learn more about Petra, please visit **abdobooklinks.com** or scan this QR code. These links are routinely monitored and updated to provide the most current information available.

OXFORD FREE PUBLIC LIBRARY
339 MAIN STREET
OXFORD, MA 01540